globe-trotters CLUB

Australia

Sean McCollum

Carolrhoda Books, Inc. / Minneapolis

3096683

Photo Acknowledgments

Photos, maps, and artworks are used courtesy of: John Erste, pp. 1, 2–3, 7, 14–15, 38–39, 42–43; Laura Westlund, pp. 4–5, 13, 16; Tom Stack & Associates, pp. 6 [© Manfred Gottschalk], 13 (left) [© Dave Fleetham], 40 [© Chip Isenhart]; © Bill Bachman, pp. 7 (right), 8 (right), 9, 10 (left), 15 (left), 20 (top), 23 (both), 24, 30, 31 (left), 32 (bottom), 33, 35 (right), 36 (left), 37 (right), 43; © Superstock, pp. 7 (left), 11 (right), 12 (left), 19 (right), 29 (top), 43; Australian Tourism Commission, pp. 8 (left), 28, 29 (bottom), 31 (right), 42 [Kata Tjuta], (right), 44; © Images International/ Erwin C. "Bud" Nelsen, pp. 11 (left), 26, 34; © Betty Crowell, pp. 12 (right), 36–37, 45; Tourism Australia, p. 13 (right); © Don Eastman, p. 14; © Peter Holden/Visuals Unlimited, p. 15 (right); © TRIP/Eric Smith, pp. 17, 18, 20 (left), 25, 32 (top), 38; © TRIP/H. Rogers, p. 19 (top); Buddy Mays/TRAVEL STOCK, p. 21; © Walt Anderson/ Visuals Unlimited, p. 22; ©TRIP/Trip p. 27; Minneapolis Public Library and Information Center, p. 35 (left); © TRIP/J. Cox, p. 39; Max B. Miller/Fotos International/ Archive Photos, p. 41. Cover photo of Sydney Opera House, © TRIP/Eric Smith.

Copyright © 1999 by Sean McCollum

All rights reserved. International copyright secured. No part of this book may be reproduced, stored in a retrieval system, or transmitted in any form or by any means—electronic, mechanical, photocopying, recording, or otherwise—without the prior written permission of Carolrhoda Books, Inc., except for the inclusion of brief quotations in an acknowledged review.

Carolrhoda Books, Inc.
c/o The Lerner Publishing Group
241 First Avenue North
Minneapolis, Minnesota 55401 U.S.A.

Website address: www.lernerbooks.com

Words in **bold type** are explained in a glossary that begins on page 44.

Library of Congress Cataloging-in-Publication Data

McCollum, Sean
    Australia/ by Sean McCollum
       p.   cm. — (Globe-trotters club)
    Includes index.
    Summary: An overview of Australia emphasizing its cultural aspects.
    ISBN 1–57505–104–4 (lib. bdg. : alk. paper)
    Australia—Juvenile literature. [1. Australia.] I. Title II. Series:
Globe-trotters club (Series)
DU96.M29 1999
994—DC21   97-18774

Manufactured in the United States of America
1 2 3 4 5 6 – JR – 04 03 02 01 00 99

Contents

Welcome to Australia!	4	Party Time	28
Cake and Bones	6	Sports Fanatics	30
Slip, Slap, Slop	8	Aussie Tucker	32
Aussie Animals	10	Off to School	34
A Giant Aquarium	12	Going On Holiday	36
First Australians	14	Australian Doodles	38
Becoming Australia	16	That's Showbiz	40
City Living	18	Crack a Book	42
Country Aussies	20	*Glossary*	44
Home Again	22	*Pronunciation Guide*	46
Speaking Strine	24	*Further Reading*	47
Faith Down Under	26	*Index*	48

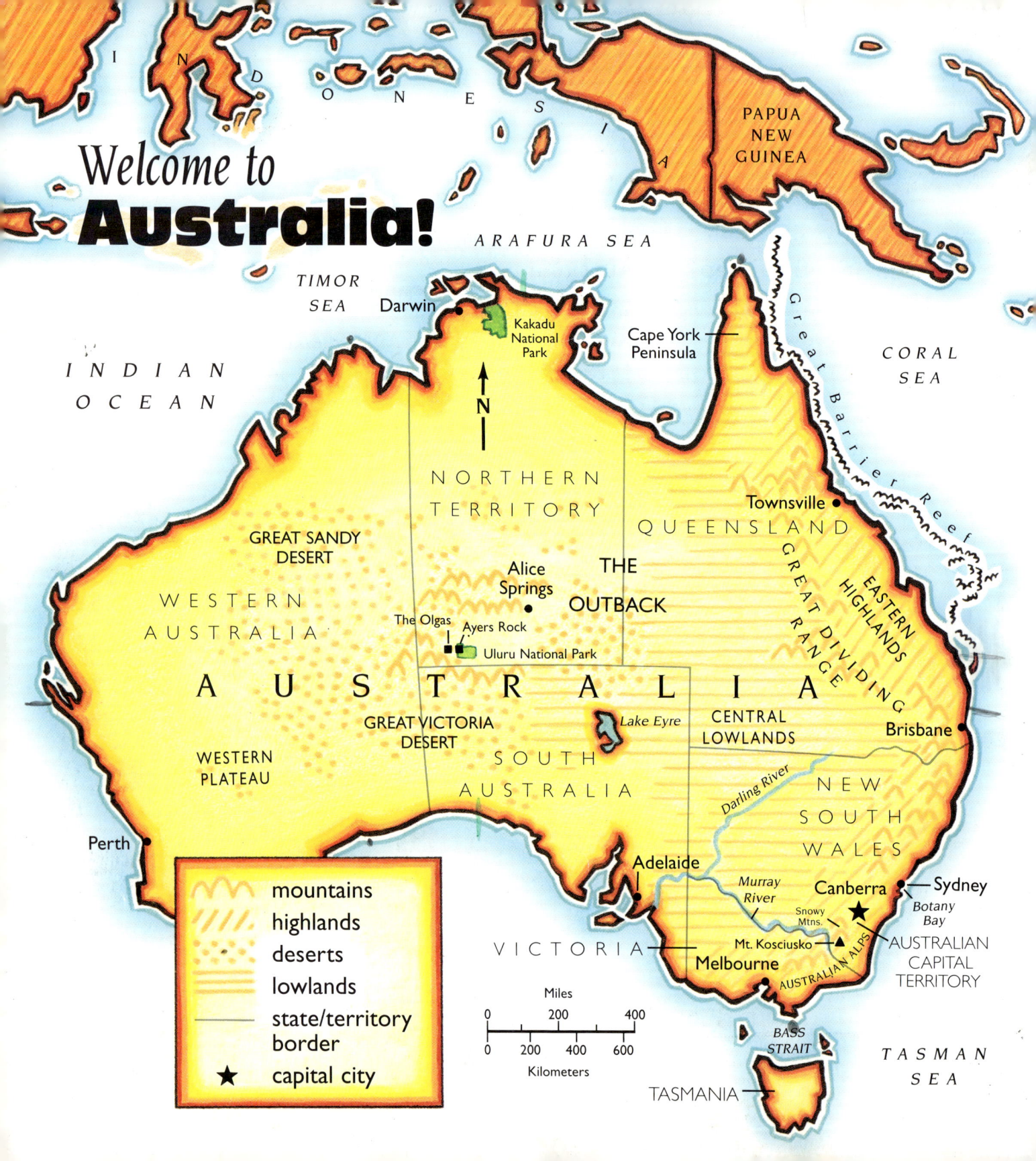

Welcome to Australia!

INDONESIA

PAPUA NEW GUINEA

ARAFURA SEA

TIMOR SEA

Darwin

Kakadu National Park

Cape York Peninsula

CORAL SEA

INDIAN OCEAN

N

NORTHERN TERRITORY

GREAT SANDY DESERT

QUEENSLAND

Townsville

Great Barrier Reef

WESTERN AUSTRALIA

Alice Springs

THE OUTBACK

The Olgas · Ayers Rock
Uluru National Park

EASTERN HIGHLANDS

GREAT DIVIDING RANGE

A U S T R A L I A

GREAT VICTORIA DESERT

Lake Eyre

CENTRAL LOWLANDS

Brisbane

WESTERN PLATEAU

SOUTH AUSTRALIA

Darling River

NEW SOUTH WALES

Perth

Adelaide

Murray River

Canberra ★ — Sydney
Botany Bay

Snowy Mtns.

VICTORIA

Mt. Kosciusko ▲

AUSTRALIAN ALPS

AUSTRALIAN CAPITAL TERRITORY

Melbourne

Miles
0 200 400
0 200 400 600
Kilometers

BASS STRAIT

TASMAN SEA

TASMANIA

Legend:
- 〰️ mountains
- ╱╱╱ highlands
- ∴∴∴ deserts
- ≡≡≡ lowlands
- —— state/territory border
- ★ capital city

Where in the world can you find an island, a **continent,** and a country all at the same time? Australia! Look at the map of Australia. There's water—two oceans and four seas—on all sides. To the east is the vast Pacific Ocean. To the south and west lies the Indian Ocean. The Tasman Sea cuts between Australia and New Zealand. And the beautiful Coral Sea washes against Australia's northwestern coast. The Timor Sea and the Arafura Sea separate Australia from Indonesia and from Papua New Guinea, Australia's closest neighbor to the north.

Australia is the smallest of the world's seven continents. It has six states and two territories. Five of the six states—Queensland, New South Wales, Victoria, South Australia, and Western Australia—are on the continent. The sixth state is Tasmania, an island off the coast of New South Wales. The Northern Territory sits in north central Australia. The Australian Capital Territory in southeastern Australia includes the country's capital city of Canberra.

PACIFIC OCEAN

NEW ZEALAND

Fast Facts about Australia

Name: Commonwealth of Australia
Area: 2.97 million square miles
Main Landforms: Australian Alps, Cape York Peninsula, Darling River, Great Dividing Range, Great Sandy Desert, Great Victoria Desert, MacDonnell Ranges, Murray River, Nullarbor Plain
Highest Point: Mount Kosciusko (7,310 feet)
Lowest Point: Lake Eyre (52 feet below sea level)
Animals: Cockatoo, emu, kangaroo, koala, platypus, tasmanian devil, wombat
Capital City: Canberra
Other Major Cities: Sydney, Melbourne, Perth, Adelaide, Brisbane, Darwin
Official Language: English
Money Unit: Dollar

This is the view you'd get if you flew in a plane over Australia's Great Dividing Range. Look out below!

Cake and **Bones**

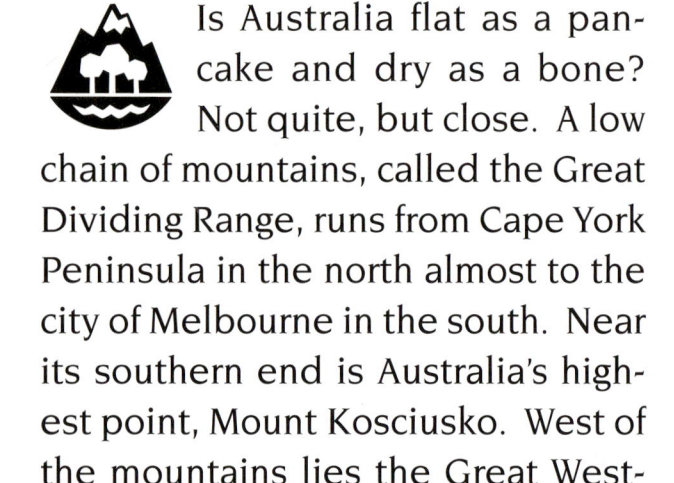

Is Australia flat as a pancake and dry as a bone? Not quite, but close. A low chain of mountains, called the Great Dividing Range, runs from Cape York Peninsula in the north almost to the city of Melbourne in the south. Near its southern end is Australia's highest point, Mount Kosciusko. West of the mountains lies the Great Western **Plateau.**

More than half of Australia is **desert,** which Australians call "the outback." This dry land stretches from the western coast across the center of the continent and includes the Great Sandy and Great Victoria Deserts. Not all of Australia is parched, though. The strip of land along Australia's eastern coast, known as the Eastern Highlands, is where most farmers grow crops like beets, wheat, and grapes.

Farther inland lie the grass-covered Central Lowlands. Here, millions of sheep and cows graze on huge ranches. The Central Lowlands are drier than the highlands, but pumps bring up plenty of underground water to satisfy thirsty animals.

Munch, munch, munch! Sheep (above) **enjoy a grassy lunch on a hillside in the Central Lowlands. A harvester** (right) **clips a bunch of ripe grapes from vines in the Eastern Highlands.**

On the Move

Australia's deserts and huge open spaces make it tough to get around. In 1860 settlers brought camels to Australia because they adapted to the outback's harsh conditions better than horses could. These days thousands of camels, called "ships of the desert," still roam there and take tourists on adventures.

But Australia's transportation system has come a long way since the camel. Railroads and highways connect all of the major cities. Almost every family owns at least one car. Giant trucks haul goods from one part of the country to another, while railways move products like minerals and grain.

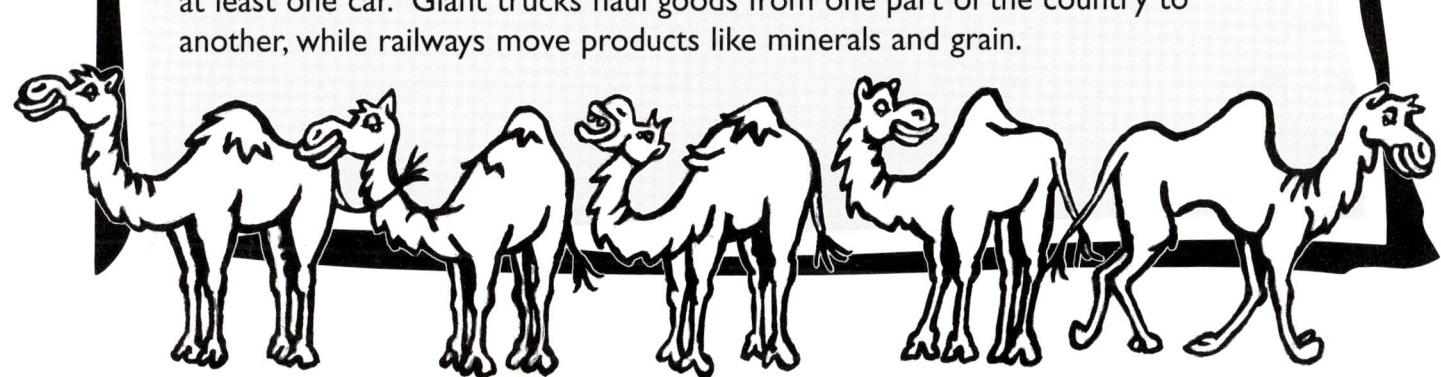

Australians may call themselves Aussies

Slip, Slap, **Slop**

Australia sits in the **Southern Hemisphere**—that's the half of the earth that lies south of the **equator.** The equator is an imaginary line that circles the earth at its center and divides the globe into two halves. Australia is often called the Land Down Under because of its location. In fact, the word *australia* means "southern place." Seasons in the

While these Aussie kids (above) **enjoy snowballs and skiing, you are probably having fun by the pool!** Seasons in "Oz" are the opposite of those in the United States. In the summer, the sun "down under" gets mighty hot. A dip in the ocean (left) **would keep you cool.**

8

and their country Oz or the Land Down Under.

Southern Hemisphere are the opposite of those in the **Northern Hemisphere.** In other words, when it's summer north of the equator, it's winter south of the equator.

At one time or another during the year, Australians experience every kind of weather. In the winter months of June, July, and August, there's snow in the southern mountains. Winters in Sydney and Melbourne are often cool and dreary, with temperatures ranging from 42°F to 62°F.

In summer the Australian outback becomes even hotter and drier than usual. Daily high temperatures hover around 100°F! Many Australians, or Aussies as they call themselves, need protection from the dazzling hot sunshine. It can cause bad sunburns and heat stroke. They even have a saying to remind themselves of what to do: "Slip, slap, slop—slip on a shirt, slap on a hat, and slop on some sunscreen."

Slap on that hat, mate!

9

Camel, wombat (an Australian marsupial), and kangaroo crossing? Australian travelers have to look out for some unusual animals.

Aussie Animals

Australia is home to many cool critters. Kangaroos, koala bears, and platypuses all live there. The kangaroo is the star of Australia's animal kingdom. Kangaroos are part of the marsupial family. Marsupials are mammals that carry their young in a pouch on their belly. Kangaroos hop through the forests and grasslands of southern and eastern Australia.

The koala bear isn't really a bear. It's a cousin of the kangaroo. Koalas are marsupials, too. And they love to eat the leaves off of trees native to Australia called eucalyptus. The tree's oil-rich leaves—the very same leaves that are used to make cough drops—are a great source of nutrition for koalas. Eucalyptus trees thrive in dry climates—their roots reach deep underground for water.

If an animal has a bill like a duck, webbed feet like a duck, and lays eggs like a duck, is it a duck? Not if it's a platypus! The platypus is a strange-looking mammal found in rivers and streams in southeastern Australia. It has fur and feeds milk to its young like mammals. But it lays eggs like snakes and birds do.

The platypus (above) **would probably win a prize in the wierdest-looking animal category.**

Sidetrack

There are about 40 different kinds of kangaroos, including red, gray, and tree kangaroos. Red kangaroos can hop up to 40 miles an hour and jump as high as 20 feet!

A kangaroo and its joey (baby)

A green-blue coral reef thrives near the water's surface, providing swimming pools to all kinds of fish. Brain coral (inset) is a strange formation, don't you think?

A Giant Aquarium

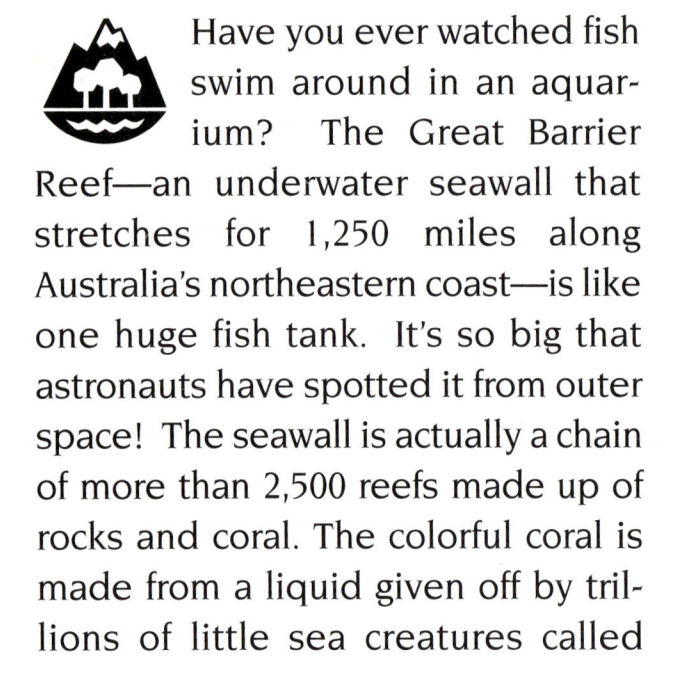

Have you ever watched fish swim around in an aquarium? The Great Barrier Reef—an underwater seawall that stretches for 1,250 miles along Australia's northeastern coast—is like one huge fish tank. It's so big that astronauts have spotted it from outer space! The seawall is actually a chain of more than 2,500 reefs made up of rocks and coral. The colorful coral is made from a liquid given off by trillions of little sea creatures called coral polyps. The liquid eventually hardens to a shell-like material. The Great Barrier Reef contains many different types of coral in all shapes, sizes, and colors. One type of coral is called brain coral. Can you guess what it looks like?

The water around the reef stays warm throughout the year. Swimmers, snorkelers, and scuba divers come from all over the world to see the 1,500 species of fish that live there. The parrot fish is a colorful creature that chews through the hard coral with its beak. Then there's the potato cod that can grow to the size of a small car! You'll also find crabs, giant clams, sea turtles, sharks, eels, and even poisonous sea snakes. Ouch!

Reef walkers get a bird's-eye view of the underwater world. They have to wear special shoes to protect their feet and must be careful not to disturb the delicate coral.

The Great Barrier Reef is a snorkeler's paradise.

Dear Grandma and Grandpa,
We spent the last two days in Brisbane. It's a fun place, right on the ocean. We took a boat out to St. Helena Island. There we walked around the ruined buildings of an old prison colony that's been made into a national park.
Today we stopped near what's called the Sunshine Coast. The beaches are huge! We went swimming, but we had to be on the look-out for jellyfish—they have a sting that really hurts!
Tomorrow we're driving to Townsville. Dad says we can take a boat out to the Great Barrier Reef and go snorkeling there!
See you soon!

13

Aborigines traveled from place to place in search of food. They used tree branches to build temporary shelters that could be put up quickly wherever they stopped.

First Australians

Australia's native people are known as **Aborigines,** which means "from the beginning." Scientists think that the Aborigines' ancestors sailed or paddled southward from Asia to Australia a long time ago. Clues show that Aborigines may have arrived nearly 75,000 years ago!

At one time, there were as many as 400 separate Aboriginal groups, including the Koori, the Aranda, and the Anangu. These people lived all over Australia. Some settled where farmland was plentiful. Others were **nomads,** meaning that they walked from place to place in search of food and water.

Traditionally, all Aborigines were hunter-gatherers. They didn't plant food like farmers but instead ate whatever they could pick up, dig up, or kill. The Aranda, for example, sucked a sugary juice found in the bodies of honey ants. Yuck!

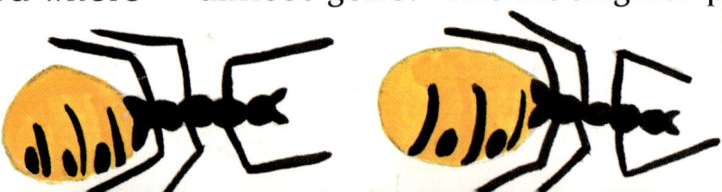

These days the traditional lifestyles of Australia's Aborigines are almost gone. The Aboriginal population dwindled, partly as a result of the arrival of British settlers. They forced Aborigines from their homes and seized their lands. Some groups tried to fight back, but their clubs and spears were no match for British guns. Other Aborigines died of diseases the settlers unknowingly brought with them. There may have been as many as 700,000 Aborigines when Europeans arrived. By the mid-1990s, only about 160,000 remained.

An Aboriginal woman teaches her young friends how to find sweet honey ants. How'd you like a peanut-butter-and-honey-ant sandwich? Mmmmm.

Culture in Danger

During the early 1900s, the Australian government seized Aboriginal lands. Children of mixed white and Aboriginal backgrounds were taken away from their families and placed with white families or in orphanages.

These days the cultural damage shows. Aboriginal unemployment and drug and alcohol abuse are big problems. But the Aborigines are gaining more control over their lives. In 1993, for example, the Australian government passed laws returning some lands to Aborigines. Australians of all ethnic backgrounds are developing more respect for the Aborigines and their traditions.

Becoming Australia

Aboriginal people had Australia to themselves for tens of thousands of years. In 1780, however, Captain James Cook landed on the shores of the continent. Cook took over the land in the name of his home country, Great Britain.

Eight years later, a fleet of ships floated into Australia's Botany Bay, near the present-day city of Sydney. About 1,500 British citizens were on those ships. Roughly half were British prisoners, and the others were British soldiers sent as guards.

Shipping prisoners to Australia relieved the overcrowded prisons in Great Britain and created a new British **colony.** During their 7- to

The Australian flag flies the British flag colors in its upper lefthand corner. A seven-pointed star stands for the six states and the Northern Territory. The right side of the flag holds the five stars of the Southern Cross—a star formation seen in the Southern Hemisphere.

These Australian kids—descendants of Aborigines, Maoris (a New Zealand ethnic group), Greeks, British, and Vietnamese—reflect Australia's rich cultural mix.

Sidetrack

Although Australian culture is filled with British and Irish traditions, times are changing. Stronger ties with nearby Asian countries have made Australians question their loyalty to the queen of England. A movement to leave the British Commonwealth and to cut all ties with Great Britain has swept across Australia.

14-year prison terms, the convicts helped to build the colony's first farms and settlements. Many stayed in Australia after serving their sentences and farmed the land or worked in city industries. Between 1788 and 1868, ships brought about 160,000 more convicts. Then other settlers came, lured by the British government's offer of cheap land. These people and their descendants are one of the reasons that Australia has such strong ties to Great Britain and is a member of the **British Commonwealth.**

These days Asians are Australia's fastest growing group of **immigrants.** Many people from China, India, Japan, Vietnam, and other Asian countries come in search of better economic opportunities. And Asian newcomers have introduced their own cultures and customs.

This wasn't how Sydney looked when Captain Cook pulled into the harbor over 200 years ago. But these days, visitors can glimpse the city's most famous landmark, the graceful Sydney Opera House.

City Living

If you were Australian, you'd probably live in a city. Australia has the most city dwellers of any country in the world. Out of Australia's 18.3 million people, 8 of every 10 live in cities. That's a lot!

Australian cities are a blend of old and new. Modern skyscrapers tower over 150-year-old buildings. With an increasing number of immigrants, and with Australians moving from the countryside to cities, **urban areas** have grown. Most Australian cities have a fairly small downtown. City dwellers usually live in single-family homes in one of the many **suburbs** that surround the downtown area.

Australia's two biggest cities are Sydney and Melbourne. Sydney is Australia's business, tourist, and cultural center. It's also its oldest and largest city with nearly four million people. The Sydney Opera House has become one of the symbols of

How'd you like to ride to school in this beauty? Trams in Melbourne are a colorful way to get around town.

Australia. Jutting into the harbor, its white, curved roofs look like seashells or a ship's sails.

Melbourne is quieter and more old-fashioned than Sydney is. Gold miners who got rich in nearby gold fields built many of Melbourne's mansions and buildings in the 1800s. But Melbourne has modern touches, too. It's the only Australian city that uses trams to carry people from place to place. The colorful cars run on rails set into city streets and are powered by overhead electrified wires. Twelve of the trams have been decorated by well-known Melbourne artists.

Greece Two

After World War II (1939–1945), thousands of Greek and Italian immigrants came to Australia from Europe. Most were trying to escape the destruction the war had caused in their home countries. Many Greek newcomers have settled in Melbourne. Only two cities in Greece have more Greeks than Melbourne, Australia!

Country
Aussies

Many Aussies daydream about a life working as a jilleroo or jackaroo. These cowgirls and cowboys herd cattle on horseback in the countryside, which Australians call "the bush." Although Australians love to visit the bush, very few actually live there. Those who do live there raise cattle and

Mail call! This jilleroo (cowgirl) gets letters, bills, postcards, and packages flown in once a week. Doctors in the Royal Flying Doctors Service visit patients by plane in hard-to-reach locations.

A tough jackaroo keeps his sheep in line, while his dog hitches a ride on the back of his motorcycle. Hang on!

It's a bird! It's a plane! It's the Royal Flying Doctors Service!

sheep, and they live on farms called stations. Stations can be lonely places, where life is very tough. Ranchers must deal with wild animals attacking their livestock and with the threat of **droughts.** Some families don't even have phone lines and must communicate by short-wave radio. Ranches may be as far as 100 miles from the nearest town. A shopping trip is a big event that only happens a few times a year.

Many roads are not paved so four-wheel-drive trucks are popular. Wealthy ranchers own small airplanes and have their own private landing strips. Kids on farms and ranches usually keep busy feeding or rounding up the animals, mending fences, or doing other chores.

Life on a station isn't too lonely, though. Families are close and depend on one another to keep things running smoothly. Kids find plenty to do.

Unlike in the bush, neighbors are never far away in Australia's suburbs.

Home Again

How big is your family? Most Australian kids live with their parents and one or two brothers and sisters. Usually Aussie kids don't live under the same roof as their grandparents or aunts and uncles. Aussie families tend to live in suburban neighborhoods in brick houses with red-tile roofs. In the hottest parts of the country, large porches provide a shady spot. Some families build backyard swimming pools to help beat the heat. In many homes, each child has his or her own bedroom. They often decorate their walls with posters of favorite sports stars or music groups.

In most two-parent Australian families, both parents work outside the home. When everyone gets home from work and school, families enjoy evenings together. After dinner and homework, parents and kids may flop down to watch the television, or telly. On weekends many families load up the car and head for a beach, a park, a museum, or a sports event. Lots of kids play football or cricket with their local sports club on Saturdays.

Turn off the telly and get to work! Two kids spend some time brushing up on their geography.

Many Aussie families still enjoy sitting down together for a meal at the end of a busy day.

23

Speaking Strine

Aussies speak English. That's a fact. A lot of British words and sayings are part of Australian speech. For example, in both countries a lift is an elevator, petrol is gasoline, and a pub is a bar. But if you overheard a conversation on a Sydney street, you might think that Australians speak an entirely different language. Aussies refer to their form of English as *Strine*. ("Australian" sounds like "Strine" when an Aussie says it.) They've got their own accent, which sounds a bit like Cockney, a **dialect** spoken in London, England. For example, "Good day," comes out like "Guh die," and "buy" sounds like "boy."

The English language has taken on many Australian words. Ranch owners are called squatters, and wild horses are known as brumbies. Outdoor barbecues are called barbies, a boy or man is called a Bruce, and a girl or woman is called a Sheila. Strine has also borrowed words, such as kangaroo and koala, from the Aborigines.

This Aussie Sheila sure looks bonzer, eh? Too right!

Aussie Speak

Here are a few Strine words and their English meanings. Try a few out on your friends and see if they know what you're talking about!

barbie	barbecue
blue	argument
bonzer	fantastic
chook	chicken
Crissie	Christmas
fair dinkum	really
g'day	good day
lollie	piece of candy
mates	friends
nicked	stole
Oz	Australia
postie	postal worker
sticky beak	nosy person
tea	dinner
telly	television

Put another shrimp on the barbie, mate!

Other languages such as German, French, and Japanese are spoken in Australia. Recent immigrants learn English in school but often speak the language of their native land at home. And about 30 Aboriginal languages are still used, although there once were as many as 250.

Faith Down **Under**

About three out of every four Australians practice some form of the Christian religion. Most of Australia's Christians are either Protestants or Roman Catholics. Marriages, baptisms, and funerals are usually held in church, but most Aussies are not regular churchgoers. Some Australians say they belong to no religion at all. Newcomers have brought other religions with them. About 8 percent of Australians are Buddhist, Hindu, Jewish, Muslim, or Sikh.

Aussies brought many things to their new country from their homelands. For example, British settlers practiced Christianity, so many of their descendants do, too.

Aboriginal religious beliefs are sometimes called the **Dreamtime.** (Many Aborigines, though, don't like this translation of the word they use. They say it makes their beliefs sound imaginary.) During the Dreamtime, Aborigines believe, powerful spirits moved about the earth creating the different landforms, such as mountains, rivers, and deserts. They also created animals and humans and gave the people their laws and customs. When the spirit creatures had finished creating, they disappeared.

Elders have the responsibility of passing on their culture. They use traditional dance and song to explain nature and history to the young people.

Muslims, who belong to the religion of Islam, pray in a mosque (place of worship).

Santa in shorts?! Remember, Australia's seasons are the opposite of those in the United States. Chrissie comes in summer.

Party **Time**

Christmas, called Chrissie by Australians, falls in the middle of Australia's summer. So Christmas cards are often decorated with Santa Claus in a swimsuit, and Christmas dinners are usually picnics in the hot sun. Kids snap open "crackers"—paper rolls that contain candy or prizes and make a popping sound when pulled.

January 26 is Australia Day, the date when British ships arrived to set up the first prison colony in 1788. Australia remained a British colony until 1901. That year Australia won its independence from Great Britain. Australia Day celebrates both events at once. Most Aussies go picnicking and watch fireworks and flag-waving parades. Actors re-create scenes from colonial days to show what life was like then.

On the goofy side, there's the Henley-on-Todd boat race held in Alice Springs each August. Alice Springs is in the dry outback, and there is rarely any water in the Todd River. So racers carry their boats along the dry riverbed. In another boating event, people in the city of Darwin compete to see who can build the most creative boat—entirely out of aluminum cans!

Aboriginal groups hold their own festivals, called corroborees, at various times of the year. Dancers paint their bodies and act out stories of magic and bravery through dance steps. Aboriginal leaders hope that by continuing such traditions, they can preserve what's left of their culture.

Aboriginal men (above) **paint their bodies, play the music, and dance the steps their ancestors did. On a lighter note, these brave Darwinians see if their aluminum-can boat will pass the float test.**

Beautiful catch, mate! In one rugby formation, called a scrum, both teams lock arms together and see which one can get control of the ball first.

Sports
Fanatics

Australians love to watch and to play sports of all kinds. Football, usually called "footie," and cricket are the most popular sports. Boys and girls at every school play cricket, a British game that's a bit like baseball. The Australian national team competes with other cricket-playing squads from around the world. For an important match, millions of Aussies will crowd around the telly to watch and to cheer on the team.

Rugby and Australian Rules are two types of footie played in Australia. Like cricket, rugby came from Great Britain. Australian Rules, on the other hand, is Australia's own brand of football. Both games are played by kicking and running a bean-shaped ball down the field. But Australian Rules is faster and rougher (and its players usually have fewer teeth!).

Soccer is a favorite team sport, and basketball is catching on fast. Australians also like to golf, a game that can be played year-round in Australia's mild climate. In summer—remember that's from November to February—Australia's gorgeous beaches attract surfers, swimmers, and sailors.

These beach boys and girls (above) are ready to catch the next wave. Swing, batter! There always seems to be a time and place for a game of cricket (left).

31

Aussie Tucker

Hungry? How about some tucker? Don't worry, it's safe to eat. Tucker is the Australian word for food.

Snack Time

For a snack, Australian kids often reach for vegemite, a dark brown paste made from yeast that tastes a bit like soy sauce. Sound tasty? Australian kids love it thinly slathered on bread or crackers.

Australians are crazy for outdoor barbecues, or barbies (not the doll, but the grill!). They cook hamburgers, sausages, chicken, or shrimp. You might be surprised by their favorite hamburger topping—a slice of beet, called "beetroot."

Want some water to wash that down? Aboriginal groups have a tradition of eating some unusual foods, including insects (facing page).

Australians start their day with breakfast, or "brekkie" as they call it. Brekkie consists of cereal, toast, and coffee or tea. Sometimes they have eggs, baked beans, and sausages, also known as "bangers." And get this—Australians may even eat spaghetti on toast for breakfast!

Dinner is often quite simple— usually meat, potatoes, and vegetables. Immigrants have spiced things up a bit, though. Greek, Italian, and Asian newcomers brought exotic recipes with them. They have opened their own restaurants, so Australians of every **ethnic group** can enjoy a wide range of tasty foods.

A trip up Sydney's Oxford Street provides a sampling of Australia's many flavors. Folks with an appetite may start with chicken feet for lunch at a Chinese restaurant. For dinner they might have lasagna and then finish up with pavlova, a traditional Australian dessert. Rumor has it that an Australian chef named his creation in honor of the great Russian ballerina, Anna Pavlova. The dessert has a whipped cream and fruit center surrounded by a thick ring of baked meringue. Mmmm, good!

An Australian brekkie in the outback is whipped up quick over an open campfire.

These students on a field trip in Sydney use the buddy system to stick together.

Off to School

Australian kids begin their school year near the end of January, when kids in other parts of the world are already halfway through. Three vacations of one to two weeks split the school year into four parts. Students have a six-week vacation beginning in mid-December, when it's summer in Australia.

Most schooldays begin at 9 A.M. and end around 3 P.M. Many schools require their students to wear uniforms. Kids study reading, writing, math, computers, and foreign languages, such as German, French, and Japanese. At 10:30 kids get a half-hour break for a small lunch called "morning tea." At 12:30 students have an hour to eat a big lunch.

Aussie students must attend school from ages six to fifteen. Six of those years are spent in the primary grades. Then kids go to the secondary level—either to a four-year high school or to technical classes to learn a trade. Australians can quit after four years of high school, but six out of every ten students graduate.

With only eight kids in this school, each student gets lots of teacher attention.

School of the Air

If you lived far away from any town, how would you go to school? Australia has solved this problem with Schools of the Air.

Kids who live on ranches, in mining camps, or in Aboriginal settlements are provided with a three-way radio. That way they can listen and speak to their teacher and classmates. They even take music lessons, playing their instruments over the radio.

Teachers visit each student's home at least once a year. Tests and papers are mailed back and forth. Occasionally students get together for a week of "school camp." One School of the Air in the Northern Territory serves an area of 500,000 square miles! It calls itself the "world's largest classroom."

Watch this split! A skier goes all out in a mogul freestyle race to the bottom.

Going On Holiday

When Australians take a vacation, they say, "We're going on holiday!" And they take their holidays very seriously. Most Aussie workers get at least four weeks of paid vacation each year. In winter they might go to the Snowy Mountains near Melbourne for some downhill skiing.

In summer Aussie kids get six weeks off from school. Many of them will probably head to a beach with their families. People of all ages surf, snorkel, and swim. Kids also have fun clowning around at local amusement parks, including Dream World, Movie World, and Wet and Wild Water Park. Woo hoo!

36

The impressive Ayers Rock is a spectacular vacation site for Aussies and foreigners alike.

Australians enjoy hiking and camping, too. Uluru National Park and Kakadu National Park, both in the Northern Territory, are favorite spots for outdoor activities. Uluru National Park is famous for its huge, red rock formations. The Olgas and Ayers Rock feature ancient Aboriginal paintings. In fact, Aborigines believe Ayers Rock is where the world began.

Please Write!

Have you ever had a friend who lives in a foreign country? It can be fun to swap tales with someone who grew up in a different culture. Why not try it? Contact an Australian penpal, by writing to:
Australian Penpal
Student Letter Exchange
630 3rd Avenue
New York, NY 10017

Spooky! An Aboriginal cave painting shows skeletons of a man, a woman, and a fish.

Australian Doodles

Have you ever written your name in chalk on a sidewalk or pressed your hand into wet cement? You were leaving behind clues of where you've been. Aborigines have made these kinds of clues for hundreds of years. They've marked sacred places throughout Australia with paintings and carvings of animals, hunters, and magic symbols.

Aborigines also paint pictures of animals, in a form called X-ray art, in which the animal's bones and organs are exposed. Aborigines of the outback are famous for their dot-painting style. The paintings are almost like maps. They show landmarks and good places to find water. These days Aboriginal art has become popular with art collectors. The Aborigines are starting to make

This modern-day Aboriginal artist practices the techniques her people have been using for centuries.

Heidelberg, a town near Melbourne) succeeded in capturing on canvas Australia's unique terrain and people. Another Australian painter, Sir Sidney Nolan, painted a series of dreamlike pictures about Australia's most famous outlaw, Ned Kelly.

money by selling their creations in small arts-and-crafts stores.

European immigrants brought their own styles of art to Australia. At first they had a hard time painting Australian scenes because the landscape was so different from what they were used to seeing in Europe. Then in the late 1800s, a group of Australian artists called the Heidelberg painters (they worked in

Ancient Art

Researchers found thousands of circles carved in boulders in northern Australia. Tests show that they were made about 75,000 years ago. That would make the drawings the oldest art ever found anywhere!

The Australian-inspired movie *Crocodile Dundee* was based on the real-life adventures of crocodile hunters like this one. Don't try this at home!

That's
Showbiz

Australians have talent all right! Aussies have been known to sing, kick up their heels, and act their way on to the world stage.

The opera singer Joan Sutherland was one of the finest sopranos ever. And Percy Grainger is a notable Australian composer whose works are based on the folk music of England, Scotland, and Ireland. Around the world, kids who study music play songs such as "Molly on the Shore" and the "Marching Song of Democracy," both by Grainger. Kids on every continent sing along with Aussie rock and pop groups such as Midnight Oil, INXS, Men At Work, Air Supply, and Rick Springfield.

Since the 1970s, movies by Australian filmmakers have made their mark on the world's movie screens. Australian director Peter Weir paved the way with movies like *Dead Poets Society*. Films set in Australia include *Crocodile Dundee*, *The Man from Snowy River*, *Strictly Ballroom*, and *Muriel's Wedding*. Australia has its share of movie stars, too. Mel Gibson, star of *Braveheart*, and Nicole Kidman of *Batman* fame, are both from the Land Down Under.

Aussie Nicole Kidman has become a major American movie star.

Tall Poppies

When Australians become successful, they can expect to get kidded a lot. They have become "tall poppies," meaning they stand above the crowd. Australians have a tradition of picking on people who they think have become too big for their britches.

Australia's awesome landscapes have inspired many songwriters and storytellers.

Crack a Book

Aussie writers helped develop Australia's unique culture. Around 1900 the short stories and songs of Banjo Paterson and Henry Lawson celebrated strong friendships and the rugged Australian landscape. Their stories valued humor in the face of disaster. Many showed sympathy for the underdog—or "battler," as Aussies say. Paterson's ballad, "The Man From Snowy River," features all of these ideas.

In children's literature, Paul Jennings and Morris Gleitzman have many fans. Gleitzman is the author of *Second Childhood*, *Belly Flop*, and other popular books. Jennings has written *The Naked Ghost*, *The Gizmo*, and more. He has won the Young Australians' Best Books Award eight times. These days Jennings and Gleitzman are combining their talents for a spooky book series called *Wicked*. In six books, *Wicked* tells the story of Dawn and Rory and their adventures with the "slobberers"—worms that can suck out the insides of living things!

Aboriginal authors tend to write about similar ideas, but each one makes his or her story a little different. For example, many tell the story of the rainbow-serpent. In one version, this giant snake created the rivers by slithering across the ground, leaving lakes where it curled up to sleep. In another telling, the rainbow-serpent's side-to-side movements pushed up the Great Dividing Range.

Young Australians can scare themselves with the *Wicked* stories.

Waltzing Matilda

"Advance Australia Fair" is Australia's official anthem. But try as it might, it can never compete with "Waltzing Matilda," the country's unofficial theme song. This ballad and others like it are important parts of Australia's songwriting tradition.

Matilda isn't someone's aunt or girlfriend. In Australia, to "waltz Matilda" means to walk along a country road. Banjo Paterson wrote the words that tell the story of a tramp who steals a sheep. Tracked down by the police, he chooses to die rather than to surrender. The last verse goes like this:

Up jumped the swagman (tramp) *and jumped into that billabong* (waterhole),
"You'll never take me alive," said he.
And his ghost may be heard as you pass by that billabong:
"Who'll come a-waltzing Matilda with me?"

Glossary

Aborigine: The original people of a land or country. This name is also used specifically for Australia's native peoples.

British Commonwealth: A group of independent nations that were once British colonies and remain under some degree of British control.

colony: A territory ruled by a country that is located far away.

continent: One of seven great divisions of land on the globe.

desert: A dry, sandy region that receives low amounts of rainfall.

dialect: A regional variety of a language that has different pronunciations from other regional varieties of the same language.

Dreamtime: An Aboriginal religious belief involving the creation of the world.

drought: A long period of dry weather due to lack of rain or snow.

equator: The line that circles a globe's middle section halfway between the North Pole and the South Pole.

Miles and miles of beaches lie on Australia's long coastline.

Australia is hopping with kangaroos.

In 1901, when Australia stopped being a colony and became its own nation, the states fought over which city should become the capital. To settle the argument, Canberra was built from scratch to be the seat of the national government.

ethnic group: A large community of people that shares a number of social features in common such as language, religion, or customs.

immigrant: A person who moves from their home country to another country.

nomad: A person who moves from place to place, following seasonal sources of water or food.

Northern Hemisphere: The half of the earth's surface that lies to the north of the equator.

plateau: A region of level land that is above most of the surrounding territory.

Southern Hemisphere: The half of the earth's surface that lies to the south of the equator.

suburb: Small housing communities that are close to a larger city.

urban area: A central city and the communities (suburbs) that have grown up around it.

Pronunciation Guide

Aborigine	ah-boh-RIHJ-ih-nee
Anangu	uh-NAHN-goo
Aranda	uh-RAHN-dah
Ayers	AH-yuhrs
brekkie	BREHK-ee
Brisbane	BRIZ-buhn
Canberra	CAHN-bur-uh
corroboree	kuh-ROB-uh-ree
eucalyptus	yoo-kuh-LIHP-tuhs
Heidelberg	HY-dehl-burg
Kakadu	kah-KAH-doo
Kosciusko	kahs-see-YUHS-koh
marsupial	mahr-SOO-pee-uhl
Melbourne	MEHL-burn
meringue	muh-RANG
Papua New Guinea	PAHP-yoo-wuh noo GIH-nee
pavlova	PAH-vluh-vuh
platypus	PLAHT-ih-pus
polyp	PAH-luhp
Sikh	SEEK
Sydney	SIHD-nee
Uluru	OO-loo-roo

Further Reading

Australia in Pictures. Minneapolis: Lerner Publications Company, 1997.

Bickman, Connie. *Australia.* Edina, MN: Adbo & Daughters Publishing, 1994.

Browne, Rollo. *A Family in Australia.* Minneapolis: Lerner Publications Company, 1987.

Cobb, Vicki. *This Place is Lonely.* New York: Walker and Company, 1991.

Dolce, Laura. *Australia.* Philadelphia, PA: Chelsea House Publishers, 1999.

Germaine, Elizabeth, and Ann L. Burckhardt. *Cooking the Australian Way.* Minneapolis: Lerner Publications Company, 1990.

Johnson, Rebecca L. *The Great Barrier Reef: A Living Laboratory.* Minneapolis: Carolrhoda Books, Inc., 1991.

Meisel, Jacqueline Drobis. *Australia: The Land Down Under.* New York: Benchmark Books, 1997.

Powzyk, Joyce. *Wallaby Creek.* New York: Lathrop, Lee & Shephard Books, 1985.

Reynolds, Jan. *Down Under: Vanishing Cultures.* San Diego, CA: Harcourt Brace and Company, 1992.

Wheatley, Nadia and Donna Rawlins. *My Place.* Brooklyn, NY: Miller Book Publishers, 1992.

Metric Conversion Chart

WHEN YOU KNOW:	MULTIPLY BY:	TO FIND:
teaspoon	5.0	milliliters
tablespoon	15.0	milliliters
cup	0.24	liters
inches	2.54	centimeters
feet	0.3048	meters
miles	1.609	kilometers
square miles	2.59	square kilometers
degrees Fahrenheit	5/9 (after subtracting 32)	degrees Celsius

Index

Aborigines, 14–15, 25, 27, 29, 37, 38, 39, 43
Anangu, 14
animals, 6, 7, 10–11, 12–13, 21
Aranda, 14
art, 37, 38–39
Australia Day, 28, 29

beaches, 36
British, 15, 16–17

celebrations, 28–29
city life, 18–19
colony, 16–17
Cook, Captain James, 16
coral, 12
country life, 20–21

deserts, 6
dialect, 24
Dreamtime, 27

equator, 8, 9

families, 22–23
farmers, 6
food, 32–33

government, 15
Great Barrier Reef, 4, 12–13

Great Sandy Desert, 4, 5, 6
Great Victoria Desert, 4, 5, 6

history of Australia, 14–15, 16–17
holidays, 28–29
houses, 18, 22–23

immigrants, 17, 19, 25
island, 5

kangaroos, 10, 11
koalas, 10
Koori, 14
Kosciusko, Mount, 4, 5, 6

languages, 24–25

map of Australia, 4–5
Melbourne, 4, 5, 18, 19
mountains, 6
movies, 40, 41
music, 40, 43

nomads, 14

oceans, 5

Papua New Guinea, 4, 5
penpals, 37
people, 14–15, 16–17

platypus, 5, 11

ranchers, 20–21
religion, 26–27

schools, 34–35
Schools of the Air, 34
seas, 5
seasons, 8–9
sports, 23, 30–31, 36–37
stories, 42–43
Sydney, 4, 5, 18–19, 33, 34

transportation system, 7, 19

vacation, 36–37